WOS
WORTH OVER SETTLING

Discovering power in your worth

Let me share my journey with you!

Table of Contents

Scripture and Prayer — V

Prologue — VI

Introduction — VIII

Dedication — XII

1	I'm My Own Woman	15
2	Mirror, Mirror	21
3	From Me to You	26
4	Are You Full or Empty?	32
5	Inside My Notebook	40

Scripture

Do not let your adorning be external—the braiding of hair and the putting on of gold jewelry, or the clothing you wear. But let your adorning be the hidden person of the heart with the imperishable beauty of a gentle and quiet spirit, which in God's sight is very precious.
1 Peter 3:3-4

Prayer

God help me see myself the way you see me. Guide me, shape me, and mold me into the woman you intend for me to be. I am nothing without you.
Undeserving but you remain loyal to me. I trust you with my life lord, I hand over my insecurities, doubts, fears, desires, and challenges to you. All my hopes and dreams are in your hands. I will no longer limit you in my thoughts.
I speak life into my life. I know I am enough; I know that I am worthy.
Let your will be done. Pour into me so that I can pour into others. I pray that I can recognize what I need from this book. Thank you for working supernaturally. Amen

Dedication

This book is dedicated to all women. I want you to know that you are worth it. You are destined to be great. No matter the circumstance, don't settle for less than you deserve. Speaking from personal experience, yes, I know that is easier said than done. Know that you have a choice to have sex or wait. By no means am I telling you to wait until marriage to have sex. I just want you to know that you have the power to decide what you want. Whether it's finding your dream job, attending school, or building a relationship with someone. If you always hold the power no one can take that power away from you. Stay grounded in God's word and watch how you start to elevate. Whatever you choose, remember sex doesn't define who are you nor does it keep a man. Try getting to know that person on a deeper level. Meaning on a mental, emotional, and spiritual level. If you bring physical into the mix too soon, you will become distracted. It will be hard for you to think clearly about whether you really like this person or not. I found my worth in my singleness. During my singleness, I discovered the power in my worth. A power that only I could find from within. My downfalls, mistakes, and bad decisions were needed. I take pride in being a vessel.

I learned that everyone has a different path. It took me a while to stop comparing my life to others. For one, you don't know the measures they took to get to where they are. Embrace your path; you were created to be set apart. It's a reason you stand out from others. Therefore, your path won't be the same as your cousin, classmate, or friend. I decided to put my challenges and imperfections on paper to share with you. As you read my book, I hope to inspire and motivate you. Ladies, only you can talk yourself into your destiny.
From this day forward, I hope you start to examine yourself. Start with GOD then YOU and see what it brings. Please remember that this won't happen overnight. It will take time because discovering your worth is a proce

Prologue

I am a WOMAN who had to gain an understanding of why I was created. God placed purpose inside of me. Isaiah 64:8 says, "But now, O Lord, you are our potter; we are all the work of your hand." It was up to me to know and understand my purpose in life. I trusted and knew that no matter what obstacle or challenge I faced, I could OVERCOME it. 1 John 5:4-5 says, "For everyone who has been born of God overcomes the world. And this is the victory that has overcome the world—our faith." Who is that that overcomes the world except the one who believes that Jesus is the Son of God?

After every battle I overcame, I began to REJOICE. Even in the midst of my battle or situation I still rejoice. 2 Chronicles 20:22 says "And when they began to sing and praise, the Lord set an ambush against the men of Ammon, Moab, and Mount Seir, who had come against Judah, so that they were routed."

Throughout my journey, I had to TRUST the process. Even when I didn't see a way, I trusted that God saw something bigger and better for my life. 1 John 3:18 says, "Little children, let us not love in word or talk but in deeds and truth. Along with trusting, it is vital to be HONEST with myself. Whether it's good or bad, I had to realize that I'm not perfect and I have to accept it.

Proverbs 11:3 says, "the integrity of the upright guides them, but the crookedness of the treacherous destroys them."

Introduction

Before college, I was just going through the motions. I was still discovering who I wanted to be. In my mind, I knew what I wanted and who I wanted, but things began to take a turn. That degree wasn't for me right then.

That guy was no longer who God wanted me to be with. I was so pressed about doing things for me that I truly forgot that it's not my plan.

My college experience changed my way of thinking. I grew in so many ways. Most importantly I became closer to God. College is where my own and true relationship with God began. I didn't fully discover my worth until after college. I am far from perfect. I have made plenty of mistakes. There have been plenty of times I wanted to give up on a lot of things. Along with things I just threw the towel in. Enough about my flaws, I'll get straight to the point.

Honestly, the biggest challenge that I am facing is being a 25-year-old virgin. Yes, I know you are probably saying wow or she is perfect because I'm still a virgin. I am here to tell you that I am far from perfect. I have struggles as well. If you truly know who I am, you would know that being a virgin is a silent battle I am fighting. I know what it's like to try to prove your worth to a guy — trying to get them to see how valuable you are. I just wanted a guy to see me the way I saw myself. I'm here to tell you that you don't have to prove yourself to anybody.

Being yourself is okay. Don't operate in the spirit of trying to be perfect for a man. Operate in the spirit of trying to please God and yourself.

You and God are the only people you should be working for. Anyone or anything else will fail you. When you get into a relationship, and it doesn't work out you might become hopeless or lost. You should be made whole and complete before any relationship.
If a break up occurs or something doesn't work in your favor, you know that your destiny isn't tied to that person. Your validation isn't with them — the only person who holds that power is God. I'm far from perfect, but I am a good woman. A woman who has a head on her shoulders. One who stands for what she believes in no matter how many eyes are looking at her. Before my season of singleness, I only knew the surface of who Chyreece was but after I knew the depths of myself. When you start finding out the depths of who you really are, you won't always like what you see. There were some things I couldn't believe, but I had to learn to accept it. If you don't learn to accept the full you, you can't expect someone else to accept you either. I remember not having a shoulder to cry on at that moment, and my tears would fall into the Bible.
I had no choice but to run to God because I needed oxygen, energy, stimulation, comfort, and protection. He caught every one of my tears. He filled me up, even in places I didn't know I needed fuel in. I had to stop going to God only when I was in my darkest moments. I needed to come to him during my happiest moments as well. My darkest moments became the most rewarding moments. I was delivered through my brokenness.

Therefore, I'm not ashamed to give God praise. I know what he has done for me. He has spared my life so many times. I could've lost my mind in my brokenness. Thankful I didn't go in a different direction. I was thankful that God was the person who taught me to love me. My creator had given me knowledge on how and why I was created. We were ultimately created to serve God. As women, God created us as very special beings. He has gifted us with the ability to create life, nurture, and winning souls. Ultimately God created woman to be a helpmate. "And the rib that the Lord God had taken from the man he made into a woman and brought her to the man. Then the man said, This, at last, is bone of my bones and flesh of my flesh; she shall be called Woman because she was taken out of Man." (Genesis 2:22-23)

Here's the thing, guys who are not aligned or connected to God won't see your true worth. They won't see the power and value you have, they will only see your physical appearance. A guy should be so in tune to God that he will have to seek God to find you. Yes, you are that valuable. Meanwhile, it's your job to start working on yourself and pray over the person you desire. God will give you exactly what you asked for, so be specific. Now, please understand that you can't be so picky—picking out his hair, eye color, and all of that. Understanding the things you seek, and dedicating time and effort toward accomplishing your goal. For instance, inside qualities were more of what I wanted than physical appearance.

Challenge #1

Write how you see yourself? Do you think you are good enough? Are you worth it?

_____

_____

_____

_____

_____

_____

_____

_____

_____

_____

_____

_____

_____

_____

Chapter One
I'm My Own Woman

Initially, I didn't want to have sex because I didn't want to be the girl the boys talked about in the locker room. I didn't want guys coming to me only because they heard what I could do. I didn't want to be looked at like that. If you know me, you would know that I am a paranoid person. So, I knew to have sex came with a lot. Getting an STD and pregnancy was my main worry. I didn't want to be a teenage mother in school. But let me be clear, my stance is not a knock to single mothers, teenage mothers, or fathers. My goal was not to fall short of my own desires. The older I got, the more I just wanted to lose my virginity. I did not want it to be forced, planned or rushed. I soon realized that this was mind over matter. I was in control of my mind. The further I got on my journey, the less I wanted to talk about being a virgin. So many people would tell me, you're perfect or that must be easy for you. In my eyes, it's one of the toughest things I have been through. I can't express enough that I am far from perfect. Just because I am a virgin doesn't make me perfect. No one is perfect, and if you think you are perfect, then you really need to look at yourself in the mirror. Instead of taking pride in being a virgin I had become embarrassed by it. It was almost as if guys were okay until I said I'm a virgin. People would say that's why you can't keep a man or just simply feeding me negative vibes. Not realizing that these negative vibes were bringing me down. I was beginning to let it control who I was. It didn't become a struggle or challenge for me until I got to college and after college.

College was filled with so much freedom. Freedom to truly make your own decisions without your parents being over your shoulder. Now for some, this could be a bit scary, but to others, this may be life. But I'm here to tell you that every decision you make can either take you places you want or don't want to be. It seemed like the more potential guys I met, the harder the journey got. I would always get told "Oh I'm not ready, you're going to be crazy," "I don't have time for that," "I can't go without sex mane," or "I don't see how you do it." These experiences brought me to ask myself so many questions. Am I pretty? What's wrong with me? Is it because I don't have sex? Do I need to be more girly? Am I too fat? Too thick? Is it because I have masculine features? Why do I always get put in the friend zone? Is my nose too big? What do I need to work on? Was I too emotional? Why do I always get cheated on? What do they have that I don't? What's so good about her? Will I ever be the one for someone? Can I just meet him? How long do I have to do this? Finally, I began to see that being a virgin is something to take pride in. I knew this all along, but I lost focus. Trust, I know what it's like to lose focus. I know what temptation feels like also. Temptation is nothing to play around with especially when you know that's not what you want. For instance, I had to stop putting myself in situations that I knew wouldn't be good for me. Each time I put myself in these predicaments I had to decide. Instead, I chose to turn the other cheek and not follow through. I decided to say that I wanted to lose my virginity to someone who loves me for me. When you are experiencing temptation, you must think outside of the feeling right then. Focus on the after, which is what I did every time. Please understand that this is not easy. You must act with your mind and not your emotions. Here are the thoughts I would say to myself. "How will I feel afterward? Are we even on the same page with one another? We're not even together! Stop while you can! You are in control! "No temptation has overtaken you except what is common to mankind. And God is faithful; he will not let you be tempted beyond what you can bear. But when you are tempted, he will also provide a way out so that you can endure it (1 Corinthians 10:13)." I didn't want to lose it to someone who doesn't want a future with me. I had gotten to the point where I no longer wanted to talk to guys who weren't trying to work towards anything with me. Prayer and meditation helped me get my focus back. God is an awesome encourager, teacher, motivator, provider, and more. It was him who turned these questions into positive outlooks. I'm not saying all my insecurities are gone nor am I saying all my doubts are gone. What I am saying is that I no longer let the opinions of others determine my value or worth. I am an intelligent, determined, focus, beautiful, imperfect, flawed, supportive 25-year-old woman who is going after everything I desire. I change the things I can, and I pray for the things I cannot. I just wanted to talk to a guy who didn't judge me based on me being a virgin. At one point, I would wait a little, to tell guys that I am a virgin. I just wanted someone to see me for who I was and not just because I was a virgin. I was who I was, big nose, masculine features, virgin and all. I learned so much just by realizing my worth.

Now, I don't care if guys don't want to talk to me because I'm a virgin or whatever the excuse may be. It's not a good feeling, but I know that someone will value what I have in the future. You will cross paths with guys who have no morals or standards. Some will see your worth and still think you're not good enough. Don't get me wrong, some guys just want to get to know you, but unfortunately, I haven't crossed paths with him yet. Some guys will only want the benefits from you but don't want a relationship with you. Regardless, be true to yourself. Once the guy sees how you treat yourself, he will align accordingly. If you aren't true to yourself then how do you expect him to be. Also, know that you are in a season and you cannot expect that guy to be in the same season as you. I had to tell guys that I didn't expect them not to have sex because I wasn't. It takes a lot of boldness, discipline, and control to hold out. If you try to take someone where they truly don't want to be, it will never work, which is why it is vital to make your own decisions and choices in life. Be your OWN WOMAN. If you're not your own woman, you can't expect to be someone else's woman. Your Identity is found in Christ, not another person.

Challenge # 2

What type of woman are you? What are your beliefs, values, and aspirations?

Chapter Two
Mirror, Mirror

I was at a point in my life where I felt like I never was the chosen one, but then as my relationship with God grew, I began to realize that I have always been the chosen one. "But you are a chosen people, a royal priesthood, a holy nation, God's special possession, that you may declare the praises as of him who called you out of darkness into his wonderful light." (1 Peter 2:9) Although I may not have been chosen by man, my father, God chose me! I would get told that "I'm not ready for a relationship," "you are a good girl, but I can't go without sex," "If you had sex you would be perfect." I allowed these things to get the best of me. I started second guessing myself on if I was good enough. Deep down I knew I was good enough but hearing these things over made me think, "If I have sex, would that change things," "what's wrong with me?" The closer I became to God, I realized my TRUE worth! Way beyond the, "I am beautiful." First, I discovered that my worth had to start with God first. Then gaining an understanding of my purpose and who I truly am. I have been crucified with Christ. "It is no longer I who live, but Christ who lives in me. And the life I now live in the flesh I live by faith in the Son of God, who loved me and gave himself for me." (Galatians 2:20) Discovering who you are may seem easy, but it takes work. I began to see my TRUE image. I started to see myself the way God sees me. God sees my heart, and he sees my shortcomings. The initial step is seeking him first, which is praying and asking God to renew your heart and spirit. You must allow him to lead you in the right direction. Ask him to help you see yourself the way he sees you.

Eliminate any distractions that are hindering you from seeing yourself clearly. Point out your likes and dislikes about yourself. It could be appearance or things within your inner self. Dig down deep inside and pull from within. If nobody else in the world loves you, always remember that you must love yourself first. Of course, we want others to love and like us, but if you don't like or love yourself, you can't expect anyone else to. I struggled with self-esteem during grade school. I had a hard time with my weight, body, face, hair, and my smile. I started discovering ways I could make myself feel confident about my flaws, so I could begin to love me for me. Such as exercising, looking into fashion styles, cutting my hair or looking into different hairstyles. Do you know you were made in God's image? Do you feel like you gave something your all and you're still empty? Whether it's a relationship, job or school. Ladies, please understand that only you can determine your happiness. Happiness comes from within yourself, your interests, people that you enjoy, or places you enjoy. God is the only person that can truly fill you up, without him you will continue to fill empty. How can you pour into someone or something when you, yourself is empty? Become whole and get full first. Before you try to offer love to someone else, you must be whole first. We all have a void that we want to fill. Whether it be from having an absent family member, heartbreak, death of a family member, or trauma. There are many things you can seek that can help you fill this void. Now if you want to fill your void correctly, you must go to God directly. Ask him to make you whole and ask him to fill you up. When you're full of him, you won't have to seek outside sources. I learned that you could do all you can, and still not be good enough for a man. Which pretty much goes for anything. You can find yourself doing everything you can and still feel like you aren't good enough, and that is the easiest way you lose yourself. It's okay to lose yourself but once you lose yourself you will never want to lose yourself again. Take it from someone who did. I lost myself, not knowing what to do with me. I didn't know where to start because I had put my all into it. It's okay to give something your all, but always remember that it's not worth you. You must remember to leave room for yourself. When you leave enough space, you will then know when you have had enough.

Challenge # 3

Who do you see in the mirror? What are your likes/dislikes? Have you accepted the real you?

_____

_____

_____

_____

_____

_____

_____

_____

_____

_____

_____

_____

_____

_____

_____

_____

_____

Chapter Three
From Me To You

Ladies, I am a living witness that sex isn't the admission price for love. Respect your body; it is a temple and sacred. "Or do you not know that your body is a temple of the Holy Spirit within you, whom you have from God? You are not your own, for you were brought with a price. So glorify God in your body, 1 Corinthians 6:19-20." If a man wants to be with you, sex will not be a prerequisite to get his attention. It's imperative that you gain a true understanding of what sex can do while trying to pursue a relationship. I'm not telling you not to have sex, but I am saying be aware of what sex can bring. Sex can bring soul-ties, mixed emotions, clouded judgment, or confusion. Pregnancy and STD's can also be a factor. Sex can block and cloud your judgment from seeing the things that need to be seen. You may think you like or have feelings for this person, but you don't. Without sex, you might start to see things you didn't see at first. I personally want to wait until marriage, but my main goal is waiting until the right person comes along. Granted the right person will wait for you. Which is why I haven't experienced sex with anyone because I haven't met the guy who sees me for who I am and value my worth. Meaning, someone who wants to know what makes me happy and wants to work toward something. Now there have been some guys who have said they have too much respect for me to just take my virginity. At first when I heard that I was like wow he really respects me. But then I started thinking "who said you were going to take my virginity." The thing is, men go in thinking, I know I can take her virginity. Not realizing that the older I got, the stronger I had become. I gained self-control and learned how to put mind over matter. I will tell anybody it's all a mind thing. You can do anything you put your mind to. Now there's a difference in wanting to, not wanting to, and not believing in yourself. Society has people thinking that sex is needed for a relationship to work. Sex was created for people who are married. It brings a husband and wife into one. "Therefore a man shall leave his father and mother and hold fast to his wife, and the two shall become one flesh." (Ephesians 5:31) Therefore, it's important to watch the person you decide to lay down with. You are becoming one with this person, and your souls are intertwining. In which spirits are transferred as well, called soul ties. The more my relationship grew with God, I began to see things from a different perspective. I started to see that the men I desired were not on the same level as me. I wanted to connect with someone emotionally, mentally, and spiritually. I wanted to get to know who they were without having sex. I have talked to many guys, but just about all of them felt that sex was just something they couldn't do without. But here's what crazy, you meet a man who tells you he can't go without sex. Let's say you guys start a relationship and y'all have sex, and everything is fine. What happens if something happens to you medically or you must leave for a couple of months, and you aren't able to have sex. Do you think he will stay? Think he will move on? Or, Stay and move on at the same time? We have been missing the thing that's called self-control and self-discipline. I'm just under the impression that people don't even know what self-control and self-discipline are or just simply don't care to know. "A man without self-control is like a city broken into and left without walls." (Proverbs 25:28) We are living in a society where guys and women just want to have sex with no relations or anything. I'm here to tell you; you are better than that. You are worth more and deserve way more than that. Some don't want to build with anyone because they aren't disciplined enough to be committed. I hear all the time; I can't just talk to one person. What happens to morals? I had a guy tell me once; I'll commit to one person once I find the right person. Here's my problem with that, there's this guy who is sleeping and dating multiple people. Then he meets a girl who he is willing to settle with. Now he starts trying to fight the temptation of other girls and falls into temptation. How do you expect him to fully commit to you if he didn't practice self-control or discipline himself to be with one person? Waiting to settle down after you have found the right person isn't the way to go. Therefore, self-control and discipline are very much NEEDED. The thing is, if you never practice self-control and discipline you will still operate in your old habits. You can get the right person, and those old habits will still follow you. Hence, so many women and men are still cheating while they are married. They think getting married will fix their ways, which could have been handled during your season of singleness. Singleness is preparation. Operating in the spirit of a wife, not a girlfriend. For example, if you don't clean up while you are single, don't expect to magically start cleaning up just because you get married. Which works the same for if you are messing with multiple people while you are trying to commit to one person. You are likely to do the same when you get marriage. Therefore, it's important to take your singleness seriously. It's okay to be with one person, but if you never put in the time or work to learn, you will never be committed to one person. It will be easy to fall into a trap. Being committed to God is essential because to practice commitment one must be committed to God. You can read all the books or blogs you want and still not gain acceptance or help. Truly submitting to God is where your true help and guidance on how to commit comes from. "But seek first his kingdom and his righteousness, and all these things will be given to you as well." (Matthew 6:33)

Challenge # 4

Are you pouring from an empty cup? Do you need more fuel? Who do you get your energy from?

Chapter Four
Are You Full or Empty?

You don't find yourself in the world. "Do not be conformed to this world, but be transformed by the renewal of your mind, that by testing you may discern what is the will of God, what is good and acceptable and perfect." (Romans 12:2) You find yourself in Christ. A man will never fill that void in your heart. You won't find validation in him either. If you feel you have or will, remember you will always have to go back to him for validation. As women, we must recognize that God is the only person who can fill the void in our hearts. We tend to misuse the words; he completes me, or he's my everything. Not realizing the weight those words carry. Yes, your words carry weight. A man can't complete you. You are complete through God. "and you are complete in Him, who is the head of all principality and power." (Colossians 2:10) God wants to make you whole, so when you do find someone, you will already be whole. You are less likely to lose who you are once you are made whole before the relationship. Therefore, it's important to fill the voids that we have. A void can be an absent father, mother, bad relationship, etc. It is vital that you fill your void with God first before a relationship with someone, which is why singleness is so important. You can discover yourself while being single. Don't be afraid to be by yourself. Please know that it's okay to be by yourself. Jumping from relationship to relationship isn't healthy. Your vision will be clouded, which can cause you to make bad decisions. Your heart is still all over the place. It's important that you heal yourself after a relationship. True healing starts with God and yourself. "He heals the broken-hearted and binds up their wounds." (Psalm 147:3) The main step that we all tend to miss is never seeking God after a relationship. If you are always in a relationship, when do you have time for yourself. Time to self-examine who you are. At first, I labeled being single as lonely. Your season of singleness can shift your way of thinking. You can benefit greatly off this shift, which is why everyone should be by themselves at some point in their life. If you never take time to learn who you are, it would be hard for someone else to know who you are. Often, we ask for things we don't even know about ourselves. For instance, you might ask for a guy who loves shopping, the outdoors, or spending quality time together. Meanwhile, you don't know if you really like the outdoors like that. The guy gives you quality time that he feels is quality time, but you don't know what kind of quality time you are talking about. When you are in your season of singleness, this is a time to learn the specifics. The details of what you really like and the things you really dislike. As well as, what you can and won't deal with while you are talking to someone. I discovered that I didn't want to talk to anybody who didn't have a purpose or plan in life. That was one thing I couldn't do. I also realized that whoever I consider must be a believer in God. Some of you might take it as being picky, but it's just setting up standards for yourself. You are worth setting standards. You aren't just anybody who doesn't have anything going for yourself. If you don't have anything going for yourself, change that. You still are worth it. When you set standards for yourself, you are not just settling. You are trusting and believing that what you desire will be given to you because you are enough. "Delight yourself in the Lord, and he will give you the desires of your heart." (Psalms 37:4) It's up to you to figure out what your desires are and being in a relationship all the time will not help you get there. Take it from someone who had no choice but to learn how to be content during their season of singleness. Granted it took me a while to understand that I was single, but I wasn't alone. Throughout the day I had some moments, but my hardest moments were at night. During the day my mind was on other things, so I had no time to dwell on my feelings. I would relax at night, and that's when different emotions would hit. Since I felt alone, I figured I was, but I wasn't alone. I had to take control of my flesh and remember that God was on my side. Don't take your singleness lightly because it's a time that you might not get back. You must pray, build, discover, and learn during this critical time in your life. These four components will lead you in the direction of discovering your worth. I had to pray for guidance, direction, understanding, and acceptance. I was in a place where I felt like NO ONE wanted me, I felt alone, and I felt as if I wasn't good enough. I allowed being a virgin to control who I was rather than having control over it. Prayer leads me to a space of contentment. I became content with my season. I realized that this was a season for me to truly understand who I am and my purpose. When you know your purpose, and who you are, your life will begin to shift. Your way of thinking and actions will change. You will start walking in purpose rather than just living. Today's society love to say living your best life but what is your best life? Is your best life pleasing to God? I was at a point where I didn't want to be where I was; I wanted more. God told me, I have more for you, but I need you to stay put until I feel that you are ready. I still had some growing to do. There were things I needed to discover within myself and my relationship with God. If not, I would not be where I am at this present moment. During this season, my perspective of being single changed. I no longer viewed being single as just being single, meaning by myself. I started to see power and value in being single. Realizing that you can do a lot without a man. Although there might be some things you don't want to do, but you know that you can do it. For example, I know that I can take care of a car. The maintenance and upkeep on it. It's an ongoing process, but I know that I don't have to depend on a man to do it. You should know the true definition of independence when you get out of your season of singleness. So, when you are in a relationship, your companion will be a help to you. There was so many things I could do while being single versus in a relationship. I made goals that I wanted to accomplish while being single. I started getting things done for myself instead of just sitting and not putting in work in myself. If I'm asking my future spouse to bring things to the table, I should be able to do the same. I must reflect my own desires and prayers. This process is called preparation. Prepare for what you are ready to receive. Sitting around not investing in myself wasn't going to get me there. I'm here to tell you, take pride in who you are, invest in yourself, love yourself, and most importantly stay true to yourself! You oversee your happiness and your destiny! Only YOU can change that! If you're single, enjoy it!!!!!! Let me also tell you that I have had MANY days, nights, and moments of break down. Sometimes these moments would last for a few minutes, hours, or days. My breakdowns would consist of different emotions. I would feel sadness, fear, doubt, pressure, vulnerability, and weak. I also felt overwhelmed, anxious, and exhausted. There were many nights where I would walk in the door at home and tell my dad we need to pray. My dad would come to my room and ask me, what's going on.

I would say I can't do this anymore; this society is all about sex, sex, and sex. I also would say I feel lonely and no one wants me; I'm always the girl who gets put in the friend zone. My dad would reassure me not to give up and reassure me about patience. He would comfort me and start praying. My dad prayers over my journey helped me tremendously! After praying with my dad and we would sit and talk. We would mainly discuss relationships and sex.

I learned how to cope and handle my emotions during these moments. My family and friends were always there to help keep me encouraged. Sometimes that still wasn't enough for me. I knew this because I would still find myself breaking down even after talking with my family and friends. Don't get me wrong their encouraging words, prep talks, thoughts, and feelings helped me out. I appreciated them for always allowing me to confide in them.

God was the ONLY person who could truly understand my life. He understood that I was really struggling with being a virgin. God started to speak to me, and that's when true healing began in me. During this time, I found peace and contentment through him. I learned that it must be mind over emotions as I said before. Operating based off emotions can steer you into some dark moments. Simply because you are acting off how you feel rather than what you think, for instance, I may have a moment and become so in my feelings that I text the guy I'm talking to and tell him to let's have sex. You see that's going off my emotions. Submitting yourself to God, asking him for guidance and strength were key elements in my prayers. That's how I was able to get through my moments. My moments made me stronger, wiser and helped me grow closer to GOD. So, I say to you, don't allow your darkest moments cause you to settle for less than you deserve. Take control over your moments, don't let your moments define who you are, you should define your moments. You can get through it especially when God is on side, front, behind, underneath, and above you.

Challenge # 5

Write down your thoughts and feelings on your journey. Look back on where you started and focus back on where you are now. What are you next steps and how will you get there?

Chapter Five
Inside My Notebook

There were so many times when I wanted to give up or give in. Even when I felt like why I must go through this. I had to keep my spirit still enough, so I could hear God. I needed to get guidance and reassurance that I can get through this. I had to think of something that will keep me on track throughout the day besides praying and talking to God. I can pray and talk to God all day, but I had to think realistically. That's when I noticed that scriptures, quotes, songs, and comedy was so helpful. I needed to be reminded of my purpose and journey. I needed the wisdom to stay motivated and encourage. Lastly, I needed to laugh, laughter is good for the spirit and soul. It helps ease the frustration or pain and allows you to be free. Honestly, whenever I did either of these things it was a release of energy. I would listen to different podcasts and sermons. My spirit was able to get fed through my mediation and encouraging time. I realized that if I went too long without getting some type of spiritual, emotional, or mental feeding, it was easy for me to fall into my moments. I needed the encouraging words, God's word, life lessons, and laughter. Your spirit is valuable, and it must be taken care of properly. Always remember that the only person that can take care of your spirit is you and God. I want to share my notes of quotes and scriptures with you. A lot of them may not have where or who said the notes. Please forgive me but know that I don't take credit for any of these. Even the ones that could be something I came up with. Hopefully, it will encourage you or help you get through your dark moments. If not, I encourage you to find something that will uplift and feed your spirit.

♦ When you are facing a visible battle, external sources are at hand because they are aware. Then you have those silent battles that no one knows about, that's tougher than the visible battle because it seems like no one is aware. Don't let external sources validate you! Remember whose hands you are in. God is aware.

♦ A true friend will enter into your experience, encourage you to endure and is not envious of your elevation!

♦ Lord deliver me from those who cannot handle my elevation. Some people in your life can't handle where God is taking you! If you're tripping off what God is doing in my life now, what are you going to do when he super-size me? @mikesteele

♦ You're not a wife when I marry you; you're a wife when I find you. A wife is not the presence of a ring it's the presence of your character. Carry yourself like you're already a wife. -John Gray

♦ Be true to yourself believe in yourself

♦ Every breath is a gift; every step is grace, every day is grace!

- We go through seasons in our life so that we can get through it for somebody else
- It's better for me to be alone than with the wrong one
- Singleness is a gift, embrace it!!!
- Speak it until you see what you have spoken!!
- I'm praying for your unanswered prayer!
- That unanswered prayer is about to turn into an answered prayer! Lord, I pray that I'm able to recognize what I'm about to receive!
- Don't depend on anything that is disconnected from God
- If you seek the things, you'll miss the kingdom, but if you seek the kingdom you'll get the things thrown in
- You may be waiting on that breakthrough, relationship or job. The WAIT is preparing you to receive more than you have asked! You think you're missing out, but God will RESTORE!

- I will repay you for the years the locusts have eaten the great locust, and the young locust, the other locusts, and the locust swarm my great army that I sent among you. You will have plenty to eat until you are full, and you will praise the name of the Lord your God, who has worked wonders for you; never again will my people be shamed. Joel 2:25-26
- "My grace is all you need. My power works best in weakness." So now I am glad to boast about my weaknesses so that the power of Christ can work through me. That's why I take pleasure in my weaknesses, and in the insults, hardships, persecutions, and troubles that I suffer for Christ. For when I am weak, then I am strong. (2 Corinthians 12:9-10)
- "If you are faithful in little things, you will be faithful in large ones. But if you are dishonest in little things, you won't be honest with greater responsibilities" (Luke 16:10)
- When you use your past as a place of reference, not a place of residence, you will find that in your time of weakness, God will show you the enormity of His strength.
- Let go of things that no longer have purpose

♦ After receiving the Word, you have to live it

♦ The things you've been going through is an indication of what you are

about to step into, trust God even when you can't trace him.

♦ I'll pray for you, you pray for me and watch God change things!!

Closing

Scripture

"Finally, be strong in the Lord and in the strength of his might. Put on the whole armor of God, that you may be able to stand against the schemes of the devil. For we do not wrestle against flesh and blood, but against the rulers, against the authorities, against the cosmic powers over this present darkness, against the spiritual forces of evil in the heavenly places. Therefore, take up the whole armor of God, that you may be able to withstand in the evil day, and having done all, to stand firm. Stand therefore, having fastened on the belt of truth, and having put on the breastplate of righteousness, and, as shoes for your feet, having put on the readiness given by the gospel of peace. In all circumstances take up the shield of faith, with which you can extinguish all the flaming darts of the evil one; and take the helmet of salvation, and the sword of the Spirit, which is the word of God, praying at all times in the Spirit, with all prayer and supplication. To that end keep alert with all perseverance, making supplication for all the saints, and also for me, that words may be given to me in opening my mouth boldly to proclaim the mystery of the gospel, for which I am an ambassador in chains, that I may declare it boldly, as I ought to speak." (Ephesians 6:10)

Prayer

God, open our hearts and minds to you. Help us to recognize the things you want us to see. Create in me a clean heart oh God and renew the right spirit within me. Words cannot express how thankful I am. Thank you for breathing life into me. Thank you for keeping us out of harm's way and wrapping your arms around us. We are undeserving, but we thank you for today, yesterday, and tomorrow. I ask that you touch each soul that pick up this book. Help them to see you out of it all. Have your way, Lord. Guide them in the right direction to their purpose. Their journey may not be easy, but I ask that you give them strength and stamina to endure their journey! Amen

Made in the USA
Columbia, SC
19 November 2019